Making
Good
Choices

**CORWIN
PRESS**

The Corwin Press logo—a raven striding across an open book—represents the happy union of courage and learning. We are a professional-level publisher of books and journals for K-12 educators, and we are committed to creating and providing resources that embody these qualities. Corwin's motto is "Success for All Learners."

Making
Good
Choices

Developing Responsibility, Respect,
and Self-Discipline in Grades 4-9

Richard L. Curwin

CORWIN PRESS, INC.
A Sage Publications Company
Thousand Oaks, California

For information:

Corwin Press, Inc.
A Sage Publications Company
2455 Teller Road
Thousand Oaks, California 91320
www.corwinpress.com

Sage Publications Ltd.
6 Bonhill Street
London EC2A 4PU
United Kingdom

Sage Publications India Pvt. Ltd.
B-42 Panchsheel Enclave
Post Box 4109
New Delhi 110 017 India

Printed in the United States of America

Library of Congress Cataloging-in-Publication Data

Curwin, Richard L., 1944-
Making good choices: Developing responsibility, respect,
and self-discipline in grades 4-9 / Richard L. Curwin.
    p. cm.
Includes bibliographical references and index.
ISBN 0-7619-4633-0 © -- ISBN 0-7619-4634-9 (P)
    1. School discipline. 2. Behavior modification. 3. Life skills—Study
and teaching. I. Title.
LB3012 .C87 2003
371.5--dc21

                                        2002014619

This book is printed on acid-free paper.

03 04 05 06 07 7 6 5 4 3 2 1

Acquisitions Editor:	Faye Zucker
Editorial Assistant:	Stacy Wagner
Production Editor:	Julia Parnell
Typesetter/Designer:	C&M Digitals (P) Ltd.
Indexer:	Teri Greenberg
Cover Designer:	Michael Dubowe
Production Artist:	Michelle Lee

Contents

Acknowledgments

I give my sincere and grateful thanks to my editor and dear friend, Mark Goldberg; Faye Zucker at Corwin Press; my colleague and partner, Dr. Allen Mendler; all of the readers for their valuable suggestions; and especially to the teachers and students who have proven the worth of this material.

— Rick Curwin
San Francisco

Corwin Press acknowledges with gratitude the contributions of the following reviewers:

Pat Carlin
French Teacher
Tate's Creek Senior High School
Lexington, KY

Steve Hutton
Highly Skilled Educator
Kentucky Department of Education
Villa Hills, KY

Diane Holben
Curriculum and Academic Services Coordinator 9-12
Saucon Valley High School
Saucon Valley School District
Hellertown, PA

Cindy Viala
Assistant Principal
Sheridan Public Schools
Sheridan, AR

Michael Herman
Teacher
Mesa Verde Middle School
San Diego, CA

About The Author

Richard L. Curwin, Ed.D., received his A.B. in English and his Doctorate of Education at the University of Massachusetts in Amherst. He is known internationally for providing thousands of educators and parents with practical, proven ideas to effectively manage children's behavior in a manner that respects the dignity of each individual. Dr. Curwin is the coauthor of the acclaimed books *Discipline With Dignity* and *As Tough as Necessary: Countering Violence, Aggression, and Hostility in Our Schools,* as well as author of *Rediscovering Hope: Our Greatest Teaching Strategy.* His publication *Discipline With Dignity for Challenging Youth* provides many new concepts and classroom-tested techniques that will help educators work most effectively with their toughest students. His articles have appeared in *Instructor, Educational Leadership, The Kappan, Parenting,* and *Learning.* Dr. Curwin has presented training seminars and workshops throughout the United States and Canada as well as in Belgium, Germany, Japan, Singapore, and Israel.

This book is dedicated to my fellow collaborator, coauthor, business partner, frequent inspirer, life comforter, and best friend, Dr. Allen N. Mendler.

1

The Classroom as a Laboratory for Life

Ages nine through fifteen are a Twilight Zone between childhood and functioning adulthood.

I have devoted most of my professional life to focusing on improving student behavior, school discipline, and the reduction of violence in schools. I am the coauthor with Allen N. Mendler of *Discipline With Dignity* and *As Tough as Necessary*, both best-selling books.[1] I have also raised three children who are now fine young adults, and I experienced all of the travails those difficult years between nine and fifteen can bring. It was exciting to think that I could write a very practical book that might help teachers and administrators work with young people in school settings.

Frustration replaced excitement when I started writing. It's one thing to desire that young people develop responsibility. It's quite another for youngsters to want to be responsible.

I often tell teachers that students between nine and fifteen live in the twilight zone between being children and functioning adults. I pictured those students who sit in the back of the class, seemingly as far away from responsible behavior as they are from Mars. I envisioned them trying some of the strategies I had in mind for this project. I easily imagined the sly comments and jokes that would spread like a virus through the class, destroying the activity.

The same question replayed over and over in my mind. *Can students actually learn to be responsible through a designed classroom curriculum or set of strategies?* Responsibility cannot be learned by reading about it, nor can it be learned through class discussion. The only test for responsible behavior is conducted after the fact, by looking at the results of students' choices.

Thus, the conditions for direct teaching and learning about responsibility are not generally congruent with classrooms. This is not to say that students do not learn about responsibility in school. They learn about it every day. My question was whether students could learn to be responsible through structured class activities.

In all honesty, I still do not know the answer to this question, but I sincerely believe that students can, and should, practice skills that lead to responsible behavior. I believe these skills can be taught in the classroom. And I believe great progress can be made, even with the Martians in the back of the room, by gently yet firmly encouraging practice with the skills. After all, soon these half-children, half-grownups will be expected to be mature, responsible, functioning adults. The more tools we can give them, the better.

In some ways, learning about responsibility in a school setting makes a great deal of sense. If we view the classroom as a laboratory for life, then it becomes a wonderful place to try various experiments. Laboratories in science are safe places to try experiments, because negative consequences are minor and learning is often major. The same is true for experiments in responsibility. Lessons learned on the street could have major negative consequences, but in the classroom, the negative consequences are relatively harmless.

Many of the activities in this book encourage students to examine their behavior in the classroom and use classroom interactions as a conceptual framework. This design allows students to experiment in a relatively safe environment. Examples and strategies are offered to help students transfer learning to the world outside of school. I am proud to offer these activities and strategies as helpful steps in that direction. The more you can aid students with the transfer process, the more likely the essence of the lessons will take root and grow.

This book reflects the strong underlying belief in children that has earmarked my professional presentations and writing for the past thirty years. Young people make the best decisions they can, based on the information they have. They are not perfect little creatures; neither are they inherently malicious or destructive.

Early teenagers, for instance, may look like trouble, but that doesn't mean they are. When my oldest child was a junior in high school, I gave him permission to have a small end-of-the-year party. He invited about twenty classmates, but 100 showed up. My house overflowed with teenagers dressed in various uniforms from punk to preppie. I was uncomfortable, a little frightened, and suspicious, especially of the weirdest looking of the group.

My son and I came to an agreement that about eighty kids had to go. He asked a number of his friends to help him thin out the crowd. I was more than a little surprised to find that some of the most helpful and most courteous of the group were the boys whose appearance scared me most. I learned a powerful lesson that evening: Even adults who genuinely like teenagers can be frightened by them when they gather in numbers. I remembered times when I was a teenager that I thought adults hated me because of my age, my clothes, and the way I spoke.

How many shop owners, police officers, restaurant managers, or teachers go out of their way to make early teenagers feel welcome? Teenagers, especially, need a supportive environment with people who understand their needs and the great changes they are going through. Ask adults if they would relive their teenage years, and you will rarely hear an affirmative answer. Teenagers, even the most troubled teenagers, respond positively to teachers who care about them, who listen to them, who take a stand for them.

The issue of "rights versus responsibility" is germane to the goal of this book in a social sense. In order to have rights and to ensure that those rights are preserved, students must honor their responsibilities. For example, to retain the right to stay out until 9 P.M., an early teenager must show that she or he will get home in time or keep parents informed of any problem— easier these days when many young people have access to cell phones.

This book focuses primarily on responsibility in a personal sense. When the word is broken into its related parts, it becomes response-*ability,* or the ability to respond. Therefore, responsibility will be used here to describe how choices are made and how to understand the meaning of those choices. Ultimately, students who make good choices demonstrate responsible behavior in the social sense.

The activities presented here are designed to help students make better choices through greater understanding of their own power and their role in creating what happens to them. But like all activity-based books, the lessons require much more from the teacher. It is not enough to follow the steps. Three additional ingredients must be added to the recipe: energy, enthusiasm, and the internal passion for learning that all great teachers have. These lessons and strategies will come to life with teachers who see them as experiences to be fully felt, who understand the difference between a writing assignment called a *journal* and keeping a record of insights and personal growth. Teaching responsibility can be as dull as doing a grammar activity, or it can influence the lives of students in valuable and long-lasting ways.

OVERVIEW

The book begins with a strategy (Strategy 1) designed to introduce the issue of responsibility. The next three sessions are related to the concept of locus of control. Strategy 2 develops the general concept of locus of control and introduces students to the differences between internality and externality. Strategies 3 and 4 deal with the sub-skills of predicting and planning.

Strategy 5 presents a model for learning from mistakes— one of the great benefits of the application of locus of control. Strategy 6 focuses on effective communication, thereby increasing personal responsibility for interacting with others.

The last two strategies are related to developing the classroom as a community. Strategy 7 focuses on allowing students to design rules for each other and for the teacher. The final strategy (8) explores how students can experience more joy from school when they perceive themselves as active members of a classroom community.

There are significant differences in the way various cultures view and teach responsibility. My way of confronting this issue has been to deal with concepts and skills that are, by and large, universal to most groups. Do not be alarmed if the goal, the structure, or the vocabulary of a given strategy does not feel comfortable to you. Simply modify the words, alter the structure, or go on to the next strategy in the book.

NOTES

1   *Discipline With Dignity*, Richard L. Curwin and Allen N. Mendler, ASCD, 1993, revised 1999.

As Tough as Necessary: Countering Violence, Aggression and Hostility in Our Schools, Richard L. Curwin and Allen N. Mendler, ASCD, 1997.

2

Eight Objectives and Ten Guidelines for Using This Book

Introducing eight strategies with language and examples you can refine to fit your students as you know them.

EIGHT OBJECTIVES AND STRATEGIES

Strategy 1.   Accepting Responsibility

Students will be able to explain the meaning of being responsible for the outcome of their behavior. Students will be able to identify evaluation criteria to use in determining which situation they can and cannot influence through their own behavior.

Strategy 2.   Who's in Charge?

Students will be able to define locus of control. Students will be able to differentiate between situations that are internally focused and those that are externally focused.

Strategy 3.   The Art of Prediction

Students will be able to explain why prediction is an important life skill. Students will be able to predict the outcomes of real-life decisions in their own lives.

Strategy 4.   Take Time to Plan

Students will be able to explain why planning is an important life skill. Students will be able to evaluate and redesign their plans.

Strategy 5.   Learning From Mistakes

Students will be able to identify strategies to learn from their mistakes. Students will be able to describe how they block themselves from learning from mistakes.

Strategy 6.   Effective Communication

Students will be able to describe passive-aggressive and aggressive behavior. Students will demonstrate direct communication in real-life situations.

Strategy 7.   Rules, Rules, Rules!

Students will be able to identify classroom rules for each other that promote responsible behavior.

Students will be able to identify classroom rules for the teacher that facilitate responsibility and respect.

Strategy 8.   The Classroom as Community

Students will be able to identify elements of a classroom community. Students will synthesize an approach to make their classroom more of a community.

Students will demonstrate personal commitment to the classroom as a community.

TEN GUIDELINES FOR USING THIS BOOK

Guideline 1. Setting

In the earlier grades for which this book is designed, Grades 4–6, a teacher may wish to make some, most, or all of the material here actual classroom instruction. Teachers can intersperse this material in the usual curriculum, use strategies as issues arise, or even use this material as part of a character education program.

In Grades 7, 8, and 9, the book could serve as a guide for teachers, a source for an occasional strategy in social studies class or psychology elective, or as useful material in a time-out or after school setting. Teachers will find, I am certain, dozens of ways to use this material.

Guideline 2. Time

The time indicated for each strategy is based on a forty-minute block or period. The actual time required to complete all activities in a given strategy will vary, depending on student interest and individual classroom needs. Strategies that will probably require more than one "period" to complete are indicated. For elementary grades, there is no problem at all. Since many upper grades now use teams and block schedules, these lessons will fit the structure of virtually every school that uses blocks of forty to ninety minutes.

Guideline 3. Instructional Techniques

There are many instructional techniques available to teachers. Teachers, of course, should feel free to use other techniques with which they are familiar or that suit their needs. I have chosen to offer the following possibilities, as I consider these techniques *key* to the success of many strategies and have seen them succeed in classrooms around the country.

Guideline 4. Journals

A journal is a personal record of experiences. Unlike diaries, journals are usually focused on growth issues, problems, and insights. They can be valuable tools for learning. I suggest that prior to beginning the first strategy, you ask students to keep a journal. Each strategy has specific journal entries as part of the evaluation process. Students will have specific writing assignments throughout the strategy, but that does not preclude the writing of other entries either directly or indirectly related to the concept. Independent journal entries should be continually encouraged.

Journals are personal and contain information that students may not wish to share. When I have used journals, I have never required that they be shared with me or anyone else. Using journals in the classroom sometimes means the teacher must trust that they are being written without actually reading them.

You might ask students to keep all information they do not want to share in a separate section or to use separate pages that can be "sealed," so you can check the progress documented in the journal. Another technique is to ask to see less personal written summaries of insights and discoveries based on journal entries.

Guideline 5. Small Groups

Throughout the strategies, you will find directions to form groups of two or three. Rarely are larger groups used. For the strategies here, small groups work best. However, the group size is not written in stone. Feel free to modify the size of groups to meet your students' needs and your own comfort with group work. Many of the small group activities can be structured as cooperative learning group activities.

Guideline 6. Role Plays

Not every student is comfortable with role-playing. It helps to ensure that students have the option to select a form of role play that is comfortable. Here are some possibilities:

- Develop scenarios for the role play
- Coach those who will role-play.

Coach during the role play. With this strategy, role plays are halted in the middle or just before the conclusion. Participants then confer with a coach, who gives suggestions to the actors for improving or enhancing the role play.

Observe or analyze and comment after the role play. This works best when the student is given specific guidelines for observing and for giving feedback.

Role plays work best when the directions are clear, the time allotted matches the time needed, the goal of the role play is clearly stated, and each student knows his or her responsibility. As the classroom teacher, you know your students and their learning needs and styles better than I do. Your method of forming groups and giving directions for this activity will work better than any prewritten recipe.

Guideline 7. Teacher Responsibilities

To help maintain a sensitive and positive atmosphere, classroom rules should be established before beginning the activities.

It is usually helpful if students participate in the process of identifying the rules they want to follow during each strategy.

One very important rule is that students have the right to "pass" on any question they feel is too personal for class discussion.

Guideline 8. Responsible Behavior

This teaches self-responsibility. When students become more responsible, they make choices based on their perceptions of what is best. Sometimes, they make choices that are different from ours. Although it is difficult to support the choices we do not prefer, there are occasions when we must do so for the overall good of the student.

If teachers do not reinforce responsibility in dealing with student behavior, then students will receive a mixed message. They may perceive responsibility as something that occurs on Tuesday mornings at nine o'clock.

The underlying value here promotes an open acceptance of students as responsible people. I hope that value permeates all interactions in the classroom, not only those described in this book.

Guideline 9. Modifications

Please feel free to modify procedures, examples, instructions, and guidelines to better fit your students' backgrounds and the unique nature of your classroom. You may also change the order of strategies in any way that feels comfortable to you.

Guideline 10. Evaluative Methods

Teachers traditionally assume responsibility for judging students' work. However, work in human development requires a nonjudgmental, facilitating approach.

Understanding this principle doesn't always make it possible to follow it. It takes a great deal of effort, and constant self-monitoring, to keep inappropriate judgments from creeping in. If you find yourself making an occasional judgment, it won't greatly affect the work, but regularly imposing your judgments will harm the learning process. I do not mean to suggest that anything goes. Quite the contrary; there is a range of responsible behavior, and there are behaviors that are clearly irresponsible. I do suggest that you continue discussion and activities until you feel that students' suggestions are responsible. As a teacher or administrator, you are part of this discussion and can, and should, indicate when you feel something is beyond the pale.

I suggest that evaluation of student perceptions, student decision making, and student reflections should be avoided. You can evaluate whether an assignment was completed.

GRADE COMPATIBILITY

The approximate grade range for this book is 4–9. Having taught seventh graders, I know that eighth graders are a different species. The difference between fourth and ninth graders is truly massive. Obviously some of the language and many of the examples used in the strategies must be tailored to the grade and age differences. However, there are other differences to consider. Students from Los Angeles have different life experiences than those from Petoskey, Michigan. The more I tried to provide examples of age differences, the more I ran into other cultural idiosyncrasies that blurred my examples even further. I finally decided that every teacher knows his or her students best. *I encourage each of you to refine the strategies, language, and examples to fit your students as you know them instead of how I imagine them.*

Good luck. I hope you have as much joy in teaching these strategies as I have had in developing them.

3

Accepting Responsibility

Strategy Question 1: Who is responsible for one's behavior?

Objectives

- Students will be able to explain the meaning of being responsible for the outcome of their behavior.
- Students will be able to identify evaluation criteria to use in determining which situations they can and cannot influence through their own behavior.

Time

Sixty to ninety minutes

Overview

This strategy introduces the concept of responsibility by examining what students can and cannot control in various classroom situations. Students will learn the first step in taking responsibility for their actions is knowing when their actions can make a difference in what happens. Students use a worksheet and work in small groups to develop guidelines for determining responsibility.

Teacher Materials and Preparation

Have:
- Overhead projector
- Pen for marking on transparency
- Chalkboard and chalk or butcher paper and markers

Note: All worksheets and transparencies are at the end of the chapter. Teachers may reproduce any materials they wish.

Copy:
Who's Responsible Worksheet (Table 3.1), one for each student; have an additional copy for each group of three students.

Prepare:
Complete the *Who's Responsible Worksheet* yourself before using it with your students. Use your experience to anticipate student questions and issues related to the strategy.

Make:
- Transparency of *Responsibility Classroom Poster* (Box 3.1). You may also want to make a poster with this statement for display throughout the activity.
- Make a transparency of the *Control Chart* (Table 3.2).

Note: All of these materials can be reproduced.

Key Information

When students understand what they can and cannot influence, they are more likely to accept the real consequences of their behavior. They reduce their excuse making and, ultimately, make better decisions.

Teaching students to accept responsibility for their behavior has some risk to it. Some students may become defensive about how responsible they are in the classroom. Protect the right of reluctant students to keep their thoughts and feelings private until they are ready to share them. Whenever possible, use yourself as an example. Demonstrate that no harm will come to those who share examples that do not necessarily portray them in the best possible way.

Emphasize to students that in this activity there are no wrong answers. As a teacher, be aware that explicit and implicit judgments will kill the process.

Procedure

Show students the *Responsibility Classroom Poster* (Box 3.1). Read the statement, "We are responsible for the outcome of our behavior."

Tell students that this simple statement has been the center of debate among philosophers throughout the ages. Every psychological theory is based on assumptions about this thesis. The Nuremberg trials after World War II—and more recently the trials in The Hague related to Bosnia—tried to apply this thesis. Everyone eventually must come to grips with it.

Tell students about stars who never learned to read in school, such as professional football player Dexter Manley of the Washington Redskins. At first, Manley blamed the system, but later he faced his problem and returned to school for reading classes. When Manley was suspended from the NFL for his involvement with drugs, he demonstrated great courage by accepting his responsibility for the problem.

Tell students that the first step in the long, hard journey to accepting responsibility is to recognize the situations that we can influence by our choices. Discuss the differences between situations students can control and those they can't. Give two or three examples of each.

- Use the *Control Chart* (Table 3.2) to provide some common examples. Ask students to brainstorm other examples in each category. Record these on the transparency.
- Distribute the *Who's Responsible Worksheet* (Table 3.1) and explain the directions. In Step 1, students read each

situation to determine whether the person involved had control. In Step 2, students decide if they would feel responsible for the outcome in each situation. Students should write a brief explanation of their decision for seven or eight situations of their choice.

- Divide the class into triads. Tell students to discuss their responses in the groups. Tell each group to pick two situations that were difficult to categorize. Suggest that students pick situations they have experienced themselves, if possible.

- Ask each group to think of two or three guidelines (criteria) to determine whether the student is responsible in a given situation. List the responses on the chalkboard and discuss them. Narrow the list down to four or five guidelines.

The list of example guidelines in the *Responsibility Chart* (Table 3.3) should be used carefully. Don't allow students to rely on these examples for their answers. Reserve examples for times when your students are truly stuck, even after you've given them gentle encouragement, subtle hints or obvious clues. Remember, responsibility in these examples is a matter of perception.

Tell groups to use these guidelines to review the situations on another copy of the *Who's Responsible Worksheet.* In a discussion, ask if the guidelines made it easier for students to determine responsibility.

Evaluation

Have students write a paragraph explaining what "being responsible for our own behavior" means to them.

Ask students to apply the guidelines developed during this strategy to at least five situations during the next two weeks. Tell students to keep a record of this experiment in their journals, noting the situation, the guidelines used, and whether they decided they were responsible.

Table 3.1   Who's Responsible Worksheet

Directions:

Step 1: Read each situation and decide if the individual involved was in control or not. Mark each with either C for in control or NC for not in control.

Step 2: If you were involved in each of the following situations and made these decisions, would you feel responsible? Would you feel you had no other choice? If you would not be responsible, then who would be? Explain your answers to seven of the situations.

Situations	In Control/ Not in Control	Who's Responsible?	Explanation: Why or Why Not?
1. You get into a fight after another student pushes you in the hall or calls you a bad name or embarrasses you.			
2. You don't do your homework because the assignment is too difficult and too long.			
3. You copy a friend's test because you don't know the material and must pass the class to remain on the team.			
4. You miss the bus and arrive late to school.			

(Continued)

Table 3.1 (Continued)

5. You are late to class after lunch because you had to wait 25 minutes in line to get your food.			
6. Everyone in class is talking, but you are the one who gets caught.			
7. You didn't do the homework because you were absent and the teacher didn't give you the make-up assignment.			
8. A bunch of kids in class make fun of you for most of a class period. Finally, you explode and swear at them in front of the teacher.			
9. The teacher asks you a question, and you don't know the answer. You sit there and don't say anything.			
10. Someone throws a wad of paper at you. You throw it back.			

Box 3.1   Classroom Poster: Responsibility

We are

responsible

for the outcome

of our

behavior.

Table 3.2   Control Chart

Students Cannot Control	Students Can Control
School rules	Whether to follow the rules
Dress code	What they wear
Criteria for honor society	How much they study
Requirements for graduation	What courses they take
Architectural barriers for the disabled	Whether they write a letter of complaint or not

Table 3.3   Responsibility Chart

I Am Responsible	I Am Not Responsible
I have more than one choice.	I have only one choice.
I determine some of my choices.	All of my choices are determined by others.
I don't always have to get in trouble.	No matter what I do, I get in trouble.
There are things I can do to control myself even when I get emotional.	When I get emotional, I get out of control.

4

Who's in Charge?

Strategy Question 2: What is the difference between internal and external control?

Objectives

- Students will be able to define locus of control.
- Students will be able to differentiate between situations that are internally focused and those that are externally focused.

Time

Two class periods

Overview

This strategy is designed to introduce the concept of *locus of control*. Students explore the meaning of this concept and the difference between internal and external orientations. A class exercise allows students to apply the concept to real-life situations. Worksheets and a writing assignment help students recognize whether they can control the outcomes of their decisions and actions.

Teacher Materials and Preparation:

Have:
A large sheet of newsprint or butcher paper

Copy:
- *Internal or External Worksheet* (Table 4.1), one for each student
- *Who's in Control Worksheet* (Table 4.2)

Review:
Teacher Background Information (Box 4.1)

Note: All worksheets and transparencies are at the end of the chapter.

Key Information

The concept of locus of control (place of control) is central to the understanding of responsibility. An internal locus of control is the perception that we control the outcome of our decisions and actions. An external locus of control is the perception that we are powerless to control the outcomes of our decisions and actions.

The locus of control is based on our perceptions. What we believe, regardless of what is true, affects our sense of responsibility.

Being responsible does not necessarily mean being more internally focused. People who are most responsible understand how much influence they have in a given situation and respond accordingly. The first lesson in locus of control is to develop an accurate understanding of how much influence a student has in any given situation.

Procedure

Discuss the definition of *locus of control*—place of control—with students. Explain that if the control of a situation is within you, the locus of control is called internal. If the control of a situation is outside you, the locus of control is external.

Give students these examples:

- If someone hits your car while you are stopped at a stop sign, the locus of control is external.
- If you hit someone's car because you were fiddling around with your stereo, the locus of control is internal.

Show students the *Orientation* transparency (Box 4.2), and review the examples with them.

Distribute the *Internal or External Worksheet* (Table 4.1). Allow students time to read and complete it. Then ask students if they have any questions about the differences between internal and external locus of control. Do they understand why each example is classified the way it is on the worksheet?

Review the correct answers on the *Internal or External Key* (Table 4.3). Ask students for additional examples of both internal and external situations.

Use the following activity, a process by which students are put into pairs, to further develop their understanding of locus of control. Students are specifically formed into pairs as explained below. Then a discussion is held about their feelings related to the pairing process.

Use the following specific technique to group students in pairs:

- Have every student stand.
- Divide the class into half 1's and half 2's.
- Ask each 2 to pick a 1 to form a pair.
- Ask the class which number had internal locus of control, which had external. Ask various 1's to share how they felt. Ask 2's.
- Make a list on the board or paper of the positives and negatives reported by representatives of each number.

Examples of possible responses include:

	Positive	Negative
1	"I wouldn't be rejected because I didn't have to ask."	"I might have had to reject someone I didn't want as a partner."
2	"I got to ask the person I most wanted to be with."	"I might have been too nervous to ask the person I really wanted."

Give each pair of students a copy of the *Who's in Control Worksheet* (Table 4.2). Tell students to decide as a pair if the situation is an example of internal or external control. Allow all pairs time to share their answers and reasons in a class discussion.

Ask each partnership to write a scenario similar to the one on the worksheet. Ask four or five partnerships to read their scenarios to the class. Ask for volunteers to give their opinions about which characters felt internal control and which characters thought control was external.

Evaluation

Have students write a working definition of locus of control for themselves. Have them include examples of both internal and external locus of control situations. Read the definitions for student understanding of the concept.

Ask students to keep a record in their journals of some of the "control" events or situations in their lives over a two-week period. Tell students to analyze the situations to determine whether control was internal or external. They should record their findings in their journals.

Table 4.1   Internal or External Worksheet (Student)

Directions: Read the following examples of situations in which control is either internal or external. Then identify the remaining situations as either *Internal* or *External.*

Examples

Internal	External
You got an "A" on a test because you studied before taking it.	You got an "A" on a test because you were lucky.
You overslept because you forgot to set your alarm.	You overslept because a power outage reset your alarm clock during the night.
You did your chores around the house because you are part of a family and you feel good about doing your part.	You did your chores around the house because your parent threatened to ground you if you didn't.
You got caught smoking because you weren't careful.	You got caught smoking because the teacher had it in for you.

1. You turned in a wallet with $50 in it because you believed it was the right thing to do. _____

2. You turned in a wallet with $50 in it because your teacher said you had to. _____

3. A favorite sports team lost even though you cheered for it. _____

4. You lost a tennis match because you did not practice. _____

Table 4.2   Who's in Control Worksheet

Directions: Read the scenario, and then answer the questions.

Mick is having a bad week. Everything seems to be going wrong for him: home, work, you name it. His friends (who don't know what a terrible week he's having) decide to play a joke on him by stealing his books. Mick arrives in class without his books or homework.

His teacher, Ms. Richards, has also had a bad week: home, kids, you name it. In every class she has had so far, students have seemed to be out of control, talking back, unprepared. She is fed up.

Ms. Richards asks Mick where his books and homework are. He says, "Who cares?" One thing leads to another, and Ms. Richards tells Mick to go to the principal's office.

Mick finally explodes and tells Ms. Richards, "Just because you're the teacher doesn't mean you control my life. No one else has their stupid books anyway! I'm out of here!" He leaves, slamming the door behind him.

When the principal asks what happened, Mick says, "It wasn't my fault."

Control Questions

1. Is Mick's situation (landing in the principal's office) an example of internal or external control?

2. Are the things Ms. Richards is responding to in her life under internal or external control?

3. Did Mick or Ms. Richards have other choices? If so, what were the choices?

4. What advice do you have for Mick? For Ms. Richards?

Box 4.1   Teacher Background Information

Locus of Control

The original concept of locus of control defined people as either internal or external, that is, people were oriented to either one or the other. Later research led educators to believe that an either/or forced choice was less accurate than a continuum with internal on one end and external on the other. This new concept allowed a more precise method of determining one's orientation.

Current thinking has taken the concept one step farther. Educators and psychologists now see both internal and external as independent variables. An individual may be high or low internal and/or high or low external depending on the situation. The two scales are independent of each other.

Most theorists believe that these ratings are not static, but vary from situation to situation.

Examples

Internal:

I passed the test because I studied.

I failed the test because I didn't study.

In these examples, whether the student passed or failed the test is irrelevant. What is relevant is whether the student believes he or she is responsible for the outcome.

External:

I passed the test because the teacher likes me.

I failed the test because it wasn't fair.

In these examples, the perceptions reflect the lack of responsibility the student feels, regardless of how accurate the answers are.

For about a week before you teach this lesson, try classifying situations in your own life as internal or external. For more information on locus of control, read some of the sources listed in the bibliography.

Box 4.2   Orientation

Students in a science class are given an assignment to build a model of the solar system in a month's time.

1. Adam and Betty fail to complete the assignment.
   - Example: Internal Orientation

Adam finishes only one planet, Earth, in the allotted time. He then feels like a failure, saying, "If I tried harder, I could have done it."

   - Example: External Orientation

Betty thinks failure is not her responsibility, saying, "If the craft store had been open last Sunday, I wouldn't have been late."

2. Charlie and Donna complete the assignment.
   - Example: Internal Orientation

Donna completed the project on time, and feels good about the continued effort she made to finish the job, saying, "I really worked hard to make that model. Looks good, doesn't it!"

   - Example: External Orientation

Charlie feels the only reason the assignment was completed was that a parent helped. He says, "I was just lucky Mom is good at building models."

Table 4.3   Internal or External Key (Teacher)

Directions: Read the following examples of situations in which control is either internal or external. Then identify the remaining situations as either *Internal* or *External.*

Examples

Internal	*External*
You got an "A" on a test because you studied before taking it.	You got an "A" on a test because you were lucky.
You overslept because you forgot to set your alarm.	You overslept because your alarm clock broke during the night.
You did your chores around the house because you are part of a family and you feel good about doing your part.	You did your chores around the house because your parent threatened to ground you if you didn't.
You got caught smoking because you weren't careful.	You got caught smoking because the teacher had it in for you.

1. You turned in a wallet with $50 in it because you believed it was the right thing to do. Internal

2. You turned in a wallet with $50 in it because your teacher said you had to.   External

3. A favorite sports team lost even though you cheered for it. External

4. You lost a tennis match because you did not practice.   Internal

5

The Art of Prediction

Strategy Question 3: Why is prediction an important life skill?

Objectives

- Students will be able to explain why prediction is an important life skill.
- Students will be able to predict the outcomes of real-life decisions in their own lives.

Time

One or two class periods

Overview

This strategy is designed to improve students' ability to predict the outcome of their behavior. Students begin by playing prediction games to practice prediction skills. They design a prediction experiment to practice predicting the behavior of others. Students then apply these skills to themselves.

Teacher Materials and Preparation

Have:
- Overhead projector
- Enough dice so that every student will have one die

Copy:
- *Prediction Questions Worksheet* (Table 5.1), one for each student
- *Prediction Experiment Worksheet* (Table 5.2)

Make:
Transparency of *Prediction Experiment (Example)* (Box 5.1)

Review:
Teacher Background Information (Box 5.2)

Key Information

The first sub-skill for developing appropriate internality is predicting. Without a sense of predictability, life is perceived as a series of random events that are uncontrollable. The more skilled students become at predicting the results of their behavior, the better able they are to make responsible choices.

Procedure

Play a game with dice to introduce the concept of predicting. Divide the class into teams of two, giving each team one die. For ten consecutive rolls, one partner predicts a number while the other throws the die. Tell students to record the number of successful predictions.

Partners then switch roles and roll the die ten more times. Repeat this process for three or four cycles, if time allows. When finished, ask each partnership to report the number of successful predictions.

Develop a prediction game based on your course content. The predictions should require a moderate level of challenge that increases as the game goes on. See *Teacher Background Information* (Box 5.2) for sample prediction games for five different classes: English, social studies, math, science, and health.

The predictions can be analyzed through whole class discussion, individual written assignments, or small group discussion. Every prediction should be accompanied with the reasons for making it.

If you teach a subject not covered in the examples, use the examples as models and design similar games for your content area.

Distribute the *Prediction Questions Worksheet* (Table 5.1). Review the examples with the class. Encourage students to add questions of their own. Tell students to choose a question to use for their own prediction experiments.

Distribute the *Prediction Experiment Worksheet* (Table 5.2).

Tell students they are going to design a simple prediction experiment. Show students the *Prediction Experiment (Example)* transparency (Box 5.1).

After students have had time to complete the assignment, collect and review the worksheets. Ask for volunteers to describe their experiments to the class.

Review the results of the dice game played earlier. Ask what difference there is between predicting a random occurrence and predicting human reactions.

Ask students to answer these questions and discuss their answers:

- Which was easier to predict, the results of throwing dice or your experiment?
- Why do you think so?
- How is predicting what people will do different from predicting what dice will do?
- How is it the same?

Evaluation

Have students write a paragraph describing how prediction could be a useful skill in their life.

Ask students to record in their journals their predictions for at least five to ten decisions they will make over the next month, using the *Prediction Experiment Worksheet* as a model. Some predictions might require a long time before final conclusions can be reached. An interim evaluation comparing predicted results to actual results can be used.

Table 5.1   Prediction Questions Worksheet

Directions: Read the following examples of possible questions for prediction experiments. Use blank paper to write your own ideas for prediction questions.

How can I make my mother smile?

How can I get my brother to do a chore for me?

How will people react if I wear an outfit that's totally different from what I usually wear?

How will strangers react if I give them an unsolicited review of a current movie?

How will an elderly person react if I try to help him or her cross the street?

What would a merchant do if I paid for a purchase of $15.00 with pennies?

How will my teacher react if my homework is done on time?

What would the principal do if I wrote her or him a thank-you letter for doing a great job?

How will my father or mother react if I do my chores without being asked?

How will my boyfriend react if I ask him if we can study at home next Friday night?

How will my grandfather react if I call him just to say, "I miss you?"

Table 5.2   Prediction Experiment Worksheet

Directions: Use this worksheet to plan a prediction experiment. Record the results of your experiment, and evaluate your predictions.

1. Name your experiment:

2. Ask a prediction question:

3. Procedure:

4. Predict the answer:

5. Give reasons for your predictions:

6. Collect the data:

7. Evaluate your prediction:

Box 5.1   Prediction Experiment (Example)

Directions: Use this worksheet to plan a prediction experiment. Record the results of your experiment, and evaluate your predictions.

Name your experiment:

The surprise handshake

Ask a prediction question:

What will happen if I shake hands with my left hand?

Procedure:

*Shake twenty people's hands, half men, half women, using my
left hand.*

Predict the answer:

*Men will pull away and ask what's wrong. Women will shake
with their left hand and say nothing.*

Give reasons for your predictions:

*Men are more interested in being right. Women are more
interested in accepting people as they are.*

Collect the data:

Five men didn't use their left hand.

Five men shook with their left hand.

Five women didn't use their left hand.

Five women did use their left hand.

7. Evaluate your prediction (include why you think you
were right or wrong):

*I was wrong about both men and women. I didn't know men
and women as well as I thought.*

Box 5.2   Teacher Background Information

Prediction Games

English

- Students read three quarters of a short story and then predict the ending. This will work best if all students read the same short story. After students finish reading the story, they can write an evaluation of how accurate their predictions were and how logical the actual endings were.

- When students have finished reading a novel, suggest a major change in the story line.

  Examples: What if Huckleberry Finn had learned how to read? What if Madame Defarge in *A Tale of Two Cities* had been caught and killed by the French Army?

- Students write their own short stories without endings. They share the stories in groups of three. Individuals write short endings for the two stories that were not their own. Compare results to see how similar the predictions were.

Social Studies

- Realign the world. In small groups, students predict the results of new world alliances. You can prepare a few scenarios in advance or let the students make up their own. Students should not predict the results of their own scenarios.

  Examples: Canada and Mexico form a trade and military alliance to become the dominant North American force. North and South Korea reunite and become a powerful economic force in the Pacific region. France and Germany withdraw from NATO and the European Union to form their own military/ industrial organization.

(continued)

Box 5.2 (*continued*)

- Re-create history. Ask "what if" questions by changing historical situations.

  Examples: What if England had not survived the Blitz? What if the American Indians had rejected Manifest Destiny and stopped the settlers at the Mississippi? What if Napoleon had defeated Russia? What if Jesse Jackson or the Reverend Al Sharpton had been elected president?

- Predict the future. Choose current situations related to economic, political, or environmental issues, and ask students to predict what is going to happen.

  Examples: Who will the Democrats choose as their next presidential candidate? Will the national debt ever be eliminated? How will America satisfy its energy needs without destroying the environment?

Math

- Predict the answers to problems before calculating them.

  Examples: Guess what 345×19 or 212×19 equals. Quickly guess which is more, $3 + 7 + 80$ or $5 + 10 + 78$.

Science

  Experiments: Ask students to predict the results of various scientific experiments.

  Examples: What will happen if we drop a 5-pound weight and a 50-pound weight from the roof at the same time? What will happen if we mix red and blue paint? How about red and blue light? What will happen if we send an electric current through aluminum, steel, copper, nickel, and so on?

- Re-create science history. Invent changes in the development of science, and have students predict how the world would have changed.

(continued)

Box 5.2 *(continued)*

Examples: What would the world be like if gasoline-fueled engines had never been invented? What would happen if the human life span were increased to two hundred years? What if people could see in only black and white?

- Think like a scientist. Students pretend they are expert scientists asked to determine outcomes to modern scientific dilemmas.

  Examples: As a biological scientist, what do you think will happen if genetic engineering of plants and animals is greatly increased? As a space environmentalist, what is the best way to colonize the moon? As a surgeon, what will be the next major surgical repair procedure to be developed?

Health

- Predict the outcomes of problems related to health.

  Examples: What would happen if cigarettes were made illegal? What about all tobacco? What would happen if all drugs were legalized? What would happen if people lost the right to drive for three years the first time they were arrested for drunk driving?

- Predict nutrition-related outcomes.

  Examples: What would happen if vegetables were not a part of your diet? What would happen if your diet consisted of only high-sugar, high-fat foods?

- Predict grooming-related outcomes.

  Example: What would happen if you never brushed your teeth?

6

Take Time
to Plan

Strategy Question 4: What do students need to know about planning?

Objectives

- Students will be able to explain why planning is an important life skill.
- Students will be able to evaluate and redesign their plans.

Time

Two class periods, or one class period and a homework assignment

Overview

This lesson is designed to teach students how to develop plans to change desired behaviors or to achieve desired goals. Students use worksheets to develop plans. They report the results of their plans in class discussions and written summaries.

Teacher Materials and Preparation

Have:
- Overhead projector
- Pen for marking on transparency
- Chalkboard or easel with large sheets of newsprint

Copy:
- *Planning Worksheet* (Form 6.1), one for each student
- *Contingency Planning Worksheet* (Form 6.2), one for each student

Prepare:
Try to use the *Planning Worksheet* yourself before teaching it. List any problems you think your students might have with the planning process, based on your experience (this is an example of contingency planning).

Make:
- Transparency of *Predicting and Planning* (Box 6.1)
- Transparency of *Planning Worksheet* (Form 6.1)
- Transparency of *The Best-Made Plans . . .* (Box 6.2)

Review:
Teacher Background Information (Box 6.3)

Key Information

The second skill related to developing an appropriate internal locus of control is planning. (The first skill was predicting, addressed in Chapter 5.) The more effectively students can make and evaluate plans, the more likely they are to change behaviors. Teaching students to plan gives them control over the changes they wish to make. Students, like adults, rarely make long-term changes unless they want to.

Procedure

Begin by relating the skills of predicting to the skills of planning. Ask students to respond to the question, "How do predicting and planning influence each other?" The *Predicting and Planning* transparency (Box 6.1) offers one answer, although different student answers may be just as accurate.

Show the *Predicting and Planning* transparency. Don't try to lead students to this answer, but offer it as another possibility. Read the text aloud and discuss the importance of both predicting and planning.

Show students a transparency of the *Planning Worksheet* (Form 6.1). Review the planning steps described on the worksheet.

Ask a student to volunteer a real-life, short-term goal. The following are some possible goals:

- Earn enough money to buy a new CD or DVD
- Finish a school assignment
- Plan a surprise for a friend or relative
- Finish a task that has been put off for a long time

The following are some examples of goals that would fit in with a health class:

- Limit myself to one sweet snack a day for a week.
- Talk with my parents without getting angry at least once this week.
- Talk to my parents about sex.
- Begin a three-times-a-week exercise program.
- Avoid a party where alcohol may be in use.

Work with the student volunteers through the first two steps of the model, recording the steps on the transparency. Encourage class discussion about the process.

Distribute the *Planning Worksheet* (Form 6.1). Tell students to decide on a short-term goal similar to the examples discussed. Tell them to use the worksheet to develop a plan. Emphasize that the goal they choose should be attainable within a two- or three-day period, but no longer than a week.

Some students may say they have no goals or that they do not have the ability to meet any of their goals. This response may indicate a student who does not wish to share or is simply not motivated. Prompt the student with cues, hints, or probing questions to help him or her find at least one or two goals.

Example:

Student: I don't have any goals.

Teacher: What are you going to do after school today?

Student: Hang out at the gym.

Teacher: Are you going to play ball?

Student: Yeah. Sure. I guess.

Teacher: Do you want to win?

Student: I always play to win.

Teacher: Then you have three goals for after school—to get to the gym, to get in a game, and to win. What do you think of that?

Student: That's pretty cool.

With caring help, every student can identify goals.

Remember that the success of the plan is not related to the success of the assignment. Failed plans are a positive learning activity. (This is discussed in more detail in Chapter 7, *Learning From Mistakes.*) Be sure students understand that they will not be judged on how well the plan works, as there is no way to guarantee that any plan will work before it is tried— only that some plans have a better chance of succeeding than others.

Introduce the concept of contingency planning. Contingency planning is the process of predicting possible roadblocks in completing the plan and developing ways to avoid these roadblocks. Use *The Best-Made Plans . . .* transparency (Box 6.2) to introduce this concept.

Let the class brainstorm alternative strategies for each roadblock. The strategies should enable students to meet the goal.

Allow students time to work through their original plans. Then ask them to report on how the plans worked. Ask for a student volunteer whose plan was not successful. Emphasize that this does not reflect negatively on the student.

Example of a Failed Plan

Goal: To earn enough money to buy a new Walkman.

Steps: Ask my mother and my uncle for some odd jobs to earn the cash.

Results: No one had any extra cash or any jobs they'd pay for. I'm not working for free.

List on the chalkboard any roadblocks that interfered with the successful completion of the plan. Ask students to brainstorm strategies to deal with these contingencies. Modify the plan so it can be tried again with a greater chance for success.

As a classroom activity or a homework assignment, distribute the *Contingency Planning Worksheet* (Form 6.2). Point out the new step (Step 3) that has been inserted into the planning steps.

Tell students to develop a plan either to solve a real problem or to change something that they do. Use the *Contingency Planning Example* (Form 6.3) as a guide. Tell students you will ask in a few days how their plans have gone. Perhaps give one reminder.

About a week later, ask students for a progress report on how well the plans are going. If students are having trouble with either expected or unexpected roadblocks, the class can brainstorm possible solutions and suggestions.

Two weeks later, ask students to write a brief summary of how effective their plans were. Be cautious about collecting the actual plans or asking for information students may feel is too personal to share. Summaries can be used to check on the assignment without the risk of personal disclosures.

Evaluation

Have students write a paragraph in their journals that explains why planning is an important part of life. They should include in this explanation how planning relates to responsibility.

Tell students to use the last two steps of the *Contingency Planning Worksheet* to evaluate and redesign their plans. This can be done in their journals. Tell students to keep a record of two or three additional uses of the planning process.

Form 6.1   Planning Worksheet

Directions: Use this worksheet to develop a plan to achieve a short-term goal. It should be a goal you can complete in about two to three days, no longer than a week. Record the results of your plan.

1. State your goal as simply as possible.

   _____
   _____
   _____
   _____
   _____

2. State the specific steps for achieving the goal. Steps work best when they are specific, small, and clear. They often are accompanied with dates, times, places, and conditions.

   _____
   _____
   _____
   _____
   _____

3. State the results of the plan.

   _____
   _____
   _____
   _____
   _____

4. If the goal was not met, state the new steps that will be successful.

   _____
   _____
   _____
   _____
   _____

Form 6.2   Contingency Planning Worksheet

Directions: Use this worksheet to develop a new plan to achieve a short-term goal. Record the results of your plan.

1. State your goal as simply as possible.

_____
_____
_____
_____
_____

2. State the specific steps for achieving the goal. Steps work best when they are specific, small, and clear. They often are accompanied with dates, times, places, and conditions.

_____
_____
_____
_____
_____

3. List possible roadblocks and some strategies that can be taken to overcome them.

_____
_____
_____
_____
_____

4. State the results of the plan.

_____
_____
_____
_____
_____

Box 6.1   Predicting and Planning

The better you are at predicting, the more effective you will be at planning. Plans are based on insight into the future. For example, a football coach bases the game plan on predictions of what the other team will do. Leaders of countries do the same on the political playing field.

Predictions can help you develop an effective plan. Plans make goals become reality by providing ways for the goals to be achieved.

Box 6.2   The Best-Made Plans . . .

Goal: Finish my history report

Steps:

1. Save the time block of 7–9 P.M. to do it.

2. Work on the dining room table.

3. Have all my necessary books, resources, notes, and pen and paper.

4. Check with other family members to make sure I can use the computer at about 8:15 P.M.

Contingencies (possible roadblocks):

1. A phone call eats up the time.

2. My younger brother or sister annoys me constantly.

3. My parent insists that a chore such as taking out the trash be done immediately.

Form 6.3   Contingency Planning Example

Directions: Use this worksheet to develop a new plan to achieve a short-term goal. Record the results of your plan.

1. State your goal as simply as possible.

    To handle feelings of anger.

2. State the specific steps for achieving the goal. Steps work best when they are specific, small, and clear. They often are accompanied with dates, times, places, and conditions.

    a. *When somebody does something that annoys me, I will close my eyes for ten seconds without talking.*

    b. *I will leave the room and write down how I feel on a piece of paper.*

    c. *I will wait until I have cooled down and then discuss the problem. I will try not to criticize but to share my feelings. The garbage could have waited for 20 minutes. I will also tell him or her that I am not criticizing, but only sharing my feelings. This is what people who love each other do.*

3. List possible roadblocks and strategies that can be taken to overcome them.

    a. *Roadblock: I won't be able to control my anger well enough to do even the first step.*

        Strategy: I will reward myself with something I like if I can do it (a food treat or extra time on a computer game).

    b. *Roadblock: I will be in a place with no escape, like a car.*

        Strategy: I will do the first step and then tell her how I feel right away.

(continued)

Form 6.3 (continued)

4. State the results of the plan.

   a. *Fewer fights with sister.*

   b. *Fewer fights with parents.*

   c. *Less stress at home.*

   d. *More free time.*

Box 6.3   Teacher Background Information

Planning

When students break classroom rules, planning how to avoid the behavior in the future is the best possible consequence. Punishments like writing names on the board or assigning detention may achieve short-term behavior change, but they serve only to make things worse in the long run.

Planning is not typically perceived as an easy or pleasant activity, but its bad reputation is undeserved. Most of the negative connotations of planning are related to planning for others, to satisfy others' needs and desires. School-based, long-range strategic planning falls into this category. Even though teachers know this type of planning is part of the job, they often hate doing it.

Contrast those feelings with feelings about planning that is self-generated or done to meet personal goals. The use of shopping lists, recipes, and self-generated to-do lists are examples. Plans are tools that help us solve problems, reach goals, and have more fun in life.

Note to the teacher: This lesson is congruent with the *Discipline With Dignity* program (Curwin & Mendler, 1988 or 1999 edition). Critical thinking and decision-making skills are related to planning skills. Some educators would even say they are different names for the same concept. If you are using or intend to use any of the prepared curricula in these areas, they will go hand in hand with the planning strategy presented here.

If you are using or wish to use the *Discipline With Dignity* program, this lesson should be taught at the beginning of the school year. When students break rules, let them develop a plan to change what they are doing.

7

Learning From Mistakes

Strategy Question 5: How do students learn that mistakes can be an opportunity for learning?

Objectives

- Students will be able to identify strategies to learn from their mistakes.
- Students will be able to describe how they block themselves from learning from mistakes.

Time

One class period, and additional time for the evaluation activity two weeks later

Overview

This lesson teaches students how they can learn from their mistakes by being nondefensive and open to self-reflection. The lesson can be applied to failed plans (from Chapter 6) or to any situation that turns out worse than expected. A worksheet and group discussions help students understand blocks to learning from mistakes. Role-playing allow students to practice their knowledge for real-life situations.

Teacher Materials and Preparation

Have:
Chalk and chalkboard or butcher paper and markers

Copy:
- *Blocks to Learning Worksheet* (Form 7.1), one for each student
- *Consulting Firms Worksheet* (Form 7.2), one for each group of three students

Prepare:
Some examples of your mistakes or the mistakes of famous people (see Procedure section for more detail).

Review:
Teacher Background Information (Box 7.1)

Key Information

Making mistakes is not necessarily a bad thing to do. In fact, it is a normal part of life. Significant learning occurs through mistakes if they are examined nondefensively and with minimal guilt or embarrassment. Many of us, as we grow older, find that life's greatest lessons come from our mistakes. One way that responsibility differs from obedience is in the emphasis on understanding how our actions affect others. Making mistakes allows us to deepen our understanding of human feelings and behaviors.

Procedure

Introduce the concept of learning from mistakes. Tell students about two or three mistakes you made in your life and what you learned from them. If this is too risky for you, use either real or fictional famous people.

Examples: Basketball great, Michael Jordan, learned he is a very average baseball player. Napoleon learned not to wage war on two fronts at the same time. Ben Johnson learned that taking steroids kept him from winning a gold medal and setting a new world record for running at the '88 Olympics. Singer Mariah Carey learned that overwork hurt her success in the music industry.

Have students brainstorm some mistakes they made between the ages of eight and thirteen and what they learned from the mistakes. List the lessons on the chalkboard or butcher paper.

Optional: Ask students to rate how important these lessons in life were in their development as young people.

For example, a student may say that spilling a drink taught the student not to talk and drink at the same time. This might be rated very low as a life lesson (or very high if the student has a sense of humor).

Perhaps a student told a lie to her or his parents. The student may have learned it works out better for practical, as well as moral, reasons not to lie to parents. This might be rated as a very valuable lesson.

Divide the class into triads. Ask students to share with their group a recent lesson they learned from making a mistake. Have each group report any interesting examples back to the full group, but only with the permission of the student involved or anonymously.

Explain to the class that it is possible to make mistakes and not learn from them. Distribute the *Blocks to Learning Worksheet.* Ask students to discuss in their groups how each block interferes with learning from mistakes.

Ask a representative from each group to share with the class a response to one of the ten blocks to learning. Ask the students if they can add any more blocks to the list.

Students should record in their journals at least one strategy that they are willing to try to overcome each block.

Distribute the *Consulting Firms Worksheet* (Form 7.2). Add some situations of your own if you like. The best are not preachy or too obvious. Try to tailor them to your students' real-life concerns. Issues with peers, teachers, coaches, and parents are good sources.

Tell students that each group is to become a consulting firm. Tell groups to invent creative names for their companies. Then each group should choose one of the situations to role-play in front of the class.

Invite one group at a time to present a scenario from the worksheet. As part of their presentations, tell groups to first discuss for five minutes the advice they would give the client; then make a final recommendation to the class.

Evaluation

Tell students to watch themselves carefully over the next two weeks and notice any mistakes they make during this period. Suggest they use the strategies they noted in their journals for overcoming blocks to learning.

Tell students to record in their journals how well the strategy worked and what they learned. At the end of the two-week period, ask students to share what they learned by looking at their mistakes.

Form 7.1   Blocks to Learning Worksheet

Directions: Discuss with your group the following blocks to learning from mistakes. Explain how blocks interfere with learning. Offer some suggestions for overcoming blocks.

1. Need to avoid embarrassment
    How it interferes

    _____
    _____
    _____

    How to overcome

    _____
    _____
    _____

2. Need to avoid getting caught
    How it interferes

    _____
    _____
    _____

    How to overcome

    _____
    _____
    _____

3. Need to appear in control
    How it interferes

    _____
    _____
    _____

    How to overcome

    _____
    _____
    _____

(continued)

Form 7.1 (*continued*)

4. Need to impress friends
    How it interferes

    _____
    _____
    _____

    How to overcome

    _____
    _____
    _____

5. Unwillingness to take the blame
    How it interferes

    _____
    _____
    _____

    How to overcome

    _____
    _____
    _____

6. Fear of consequences
    How it interferes

    _____
    _____
    _____

    How to overcome

    _____
    _____
    _____

7. Fear of losing relationships
    How it interferes

    _____
    _____
    _____

(continued)

Form 7.1 *(continued)*

How to overcome

_____
_____
_____

8. Fear of being labeled
    How it interferes

_____
_____
_____

    How to overcome

_____
_____
_____

9. Unwillingness to admit that a mistake was made
    How it interferes

_____
_____
_____

    How to overcome

_____
_____
_____

10. Inability to accept responsibility for making the mistake
     How it interferes

_____
_____
_____

     How to overcome

_____
_____
_____

Form 7.2   Consulting Firms Worksheet

Directions: Choose one of the following situations to role-play with your group. Begin your role-play presentation with a five-minute discussion of the advice you would give someone in the situation. Remember to answer the question, "What do I have to learn from this?"

I borrowed one of my dad's favorite DVDs and lost it.

I ran out of allowance two weeks early because I bought stuff I needed for a school project. Now I don't have money to go to the movies.

I got caught cursing in another language by a teacher who understood that language.

I insulted a guy before I realized he was a member of the toughest gang at school.

I let my best friend copy my test. I got caught and she didn't.

I ate doughnuts for breakfast, cookies for lunch, potato chips for a snack, and French fries for supper. I'm really sick.

I rode my bike to school when my parents told me not to, and someone stole my bike.

My friend told a fourth grade student to give him lunch money or else, while I stood nearby. The principal busted us both and she called my mother. My friend told me not to tell or else.

I took some lipstick from the store where I go a lot with my mother. I didn't get caught, but the manager told my mother someone is stealing, and now I'm scared.

Box 7.1   Teacher Background Information

Learning From Mistakes

The previous chapter emphasized the importance of planning. Care was taken to point out the difference between a failed *plan* and a failed *assignment*. It is unfortunate that so often the only word we use to describe something that doesn't work is *failure*.

Likewise, calling a plan that doesn't work a "mistake" is a misnomer. However, this lesson can be used to show the positive things we can learn from plans that did not produce the desired result.

Special Note for At-Risk Students

Some students may not believe that they can learn from their mistakes. Often these are at-risk students or low achievers; they may be thinking about dropping out of school as soon as they are old enough. Sometimes, these students may not even be willing to perceive that they make mistakes.

Do not exclude these students from this or similar activities. By excluding them, you would, in effect, be reinforcing the negative image they have of themselves. They have to be given the same opportunities as everyone else in the class. For them, these activities may be especially important.

However, great care must be taken with these students to preserve their dignity and protect their self-esteem. It helps when they can see that everybody makes

(continued)

Box 7.1 *(continued)*

---

mistakes—their friends, their heroes, even their teachers. Make sure to include as examples people these students admire.

Note to the teacher: All Teacher Expectation/Student Achievement studies strongly indicate that students pick up subtle clues from teachers about how well they are expected to do. They then perform to the expected level. We do a disservice to many students by labeling them and diminishing our expectations of what they are capable of doing.

I believe it is far better to maintain high expectations (within reason) and offer support in meeting them (hints, cues, equal response opportunity, probes, teaming with other students, individualizing time frames, etc.). The more we lower our expectations, the farther behind these students will fall.

8

Effective Communication

Strategy Question 6: What do students need to know about direct communication, aggressive behavior, and passive-aggressive behavior?

Objectives

- Students will be able to describe passive-aggressive and aggressive behavior.
- Students will demonstrate direct communication in real-life situations.

Time

Two class periods

Overview

This lesson is designed to help students learn the relationship between passive-aggressive and aggressive behavior and responsibility. Through brainstorming and role-playing, students develop alternatives to these behaviors.

Teacher Materials and Preparation

Have:
- Overhead projector
- Pen for marking on transparency
- Chalk and chalkboard
- 3 × 5 cards or small pieces of paper, two for each student

Copy:
Aggression Self-Inventory (Form 8.1), one for each student

Make:
- Transparency of *Passive-Aggressive Behavior* (Box 8.1)
- Transparency of *Aggressive Behavior* (Box 8.2)
- Transparency of *Effective Communication* (Form 8.2)

Review:
Teacher Background Information (Box 8.3)

Key Information

Behaving responsibly means having the ability to express emotions in a healthy manner. Effective communication skills allow us to express our emotions in nonconfrontational ways. Students need to know that though it is okay and healthy to express *negatively toned* emotions such as anger (there are no negative emotions), it is not okay to express those emotions any way they want.

There is danger, of course, in direct communication, even if it is conducted in a nonaggressive manner. This danger makes passive-aggressive behavior attractive. The danger is that recipients of our communication may not like what we say, may not understand it, or may be threatened by it, regardless of how effectively it is expressed.

You may, for example, teach a student to express feelings directly to their source. If that student tells another teacher that he or she is bored, the student may pay for such honesty. Practice can minimize the risk.

Procedure

Introduce the concept of passive-aggressive behavior with an explanation based on the following definition:

Passive-aggressive behavior is an indirect expression of anger. When we are afraid that someone is more powerful than we are or has the ability to hurt us, we are reluctant to show our anger because that person might get angry with us.

Show students the *Passive-Aggressive Behavior* transparency (Box 8.1). Brainstorm with the class other examples of passive-aggressive behavior. List them on the transparency.

Pick out five or six of the more interesting examples. Ask students to comment on how they would feel if someone acted that way with them.

Discuss some of the possible benefits of passive-aggressive behavior (as opposed to direct expression of feelings) and some of the liabilities. List the benefits and liabilities on the chalkboard.

Tell students that passive-aggressive behavior is not the only ineffective way to express anger. Direct confrontation also causes serious communication problems. Show students the *Aggressive Behavior* transparency (Box 8.2).

Brainstorm other examples of aggressive behavior. List them on the transparency.

Divide the class into groups of four or five. Assign one behavior listed on the *Passive-Aggressive Behavior* transparency (Box 8.1) to half the groups. Assign one behavior listed on the *Aggressive Behavior* transparency (Box 8.2) to the remaining groups. Tell groups to create a role play that depicts that behavior.

Tell groups that those who are not part of the role play are observers. Their job is to watch the role play carefully. Observers will take turns evaluating how realistic the role play was and what they would do in that situation.

Put students back into the full group, and distribute the *Aggression Self-Inventory* (Form 8.1). Ask each student to list six situations when he or she was tempted to behave in an aggressive manner. Ask students to rank the situations from one to five. One is the most dangerous. Five is the least dangerous.

Give each student two 3″ × 5″ cards (or pieces of paper). Tell students to list one of the situations from the worksheet on each card. Tell students not to put their names on the cards.

Collect the cards, shuffle them, and read them one at a time to the class. After each card, ask the class to brainstorm ways to express their feelings in that situation without getting into a fight or serious argument. Write the suggestions on the board.

Tell students that learning to communicate feelings directly is consistent with responsible behavior, which emphasizes accepting the consequences of our actions. When we learn to communicate effectively, many of the things we feared will never materialize and relationships will improve.

Show students the *Effective Communication* transparency (Form 8.2). Tell groups to use these techniques to rewrite and replay their role plays, replacing passive-aggressive techniques or aggressive behaviors with direct communication. After each role play, discuss with the class the most likely short-term and long-term consequences of each scenario.

Evaluation

Tell students to keep a record in their journals of ways they express anger for a two-week period. Of course, they won't write down every little incident, but each student should summarize between six and eight incidents over two weeks. After each episode, they should answer the following questions:

- How did you express your anger?
- Did you use passive-aggressive techniques, aggressive behavior, or direct communication?
- How did you feel when you expressed anger?
- What were the immediate consequences?

Form 8.1   Aggression Self-Inventory

Directions: List six situations when you were tempted to get into a fight in the last few months—either verbal or physical. Using a scale from 1 to 5, rank each situation from most to least dangerous. Write the number of your ranking in the box for each situation:

1 = the most dangerous, 5 = the least dangerous

1. _____
   _____
   _____

2. _____
   _____
   _____

3. _____
   _____
   _____

4. _____
   _____
   _____

5. _____
   _____
   _____

6. _____
   _____
   _____

Box 8.1   Passive-Aggressive Behavior

Silent anger:
- Making a mess out of spite
- "Accidentally" bumping into someone
- "Accidentally" spilling something on someone
- "Accidentally" misplacing something that belongs to another
- Calling someone by an incorrect name
- Ignoring or pretending not to hear someone
- Talking behind someone's back
- "Forgetting" to do something you promised to do
- Doing what you were asked to do, but doing a bad job
- Losing something you don't really want, but your parents want you to have

---

Box 8.2   Aggressive Behavior

- Calling someone names or swearing
- Hitting someone
- Throwing or breaking anything that belongs to someone else
- Refusing to help or cooperate when asked

Form 8.2   Effective Communication

Active Listening

Restate the other person's words to show you understand what they said.

"I" statements

State your own feelings ("I feel angry when you . . . ")

Explore Alternatives

- Write how you feel on paper or in a journal.

- Hit a pillow, doll, or other symbolic object.

- Write a hate letter and then rip it to shreds without giving it to the person.

Stress Relief

- Put the situation on hold

- Meditate

- Breathing techniques

- A walk or exercise

- Talk to a trusted friend or family member

Box 8.3   Teacher Background Information

Passive-Aggressive Behavior

Sometimes it is easier to show our anger using indirect or passive techniques. Passive-aggressive behavior allows us to punish other people without having to take a stand and without being accountable for what we do. We usually behave this way when we think other people have the power to hurt us or when we are afraid to communicate directly.

We can be hurt by a direct confrontation in a variety of ways. For example, a parent can take away an allowance, deny love, lower her or his opinion of us, or make us feel wrong. Passive-aggressive behavior appears safer because it is indirect.

But passive-aggressive behavior does more damage over time, as it only continues the battle. The target of this behavior usually resents it and fights back (either through direct confrontation or passive-aggressive techniques of his or her own).

Terrorism is a political example at the international level. Because terrorist groups are afraid to tackle bigger countries in direct confrontation (war), they hit and run (bombing an airliner, for example), or the devastating attack on the World Trade Center and the Pentagon on September 11, 2001, in what might be called passive-aggressive methods.

I am not in any way condoning or recommending war as an alternative to terrorism. I abhor both. However, the analogy holds, and the power of the image does help clarify why passive aggression is used and how it works. If countries agreed to communicate through negotiation (the essence of this lesson), perhaps both war and terrorism would become obsolete.

(continued)

Box 8.3 *(continued)*

The terrorist analogy points out another danger of passive-aggressive behavior. People who engage in passive-aggressive behavior do so because they feel hopeless. They perceive that they have only an either-or choice between passivity and direct aggression such as fighting, violence, or verbal attack. They believe that other alternatives such as negotiation, compromise, or completely passive resistance such as practiced by Gandhi in India or Martin Luther King, Jr., in the United States will fail. This lesson is designed to provide skills in other alternatives.

Some families or cultures highly value harmony over confrontation. In these cases, passive-aggressive behavior might, on the surface, appear culturally appropriate. However, there is a critical difference between seeking harmony and expressing anger through passive-aggressive techniques.

If your students have learned that the culturally accepted way to express anger and hostility is through passive-aggressive behavior, proceed slowly and carefully. You might try to meet with parent(s) and discuss the issue. Together, you might find ways to communicate to your students the difference between harmony and indirectly expressed aggression.

Passive-aggressive behavior often appears in the classroom. When embarrassed or threatened, students often use passive-aggressive techniques to punish the teacher. For instance, the student might fumble for the right paper for a minute or two and then claim it is at home. The teacher usually responds to the students' payback with more of the behavior that started the problem. The situation worsens as both sides struggle to maintain their dignity.

(continued)

Box 8.3 *(continued)*

The best solution is for teachers to treat students with dignity at all times. However, this is a high standard that occasionally is not met. If students can communicate directly, there is a better chance that the cycle will stop before it gets up a full head of steam.

It is usually more helpful to tell people, as directly as possible, what we are angry about, what is bothering us and why. Being direct takes more courage. But in the long run, it makes us feel better, and it tells the target person exactly what we want.

9

Rules, Rules, Rules!

Strategy Question 7: How do students and teachers formulate classroom rules that promote responsibility and respect?

Objectives

- Students will be able to identify classroom rules for each other that promote responsible behavior.
- Students will be able to identify classroom rules for the teacher that facilitate responsibility and respect.

Time

One class period, and additional time for the evaluation activity about one month later.

Overview

This lesson begins the process of developing a classroom community by having students develop rules for each other and for the teacher. Students work in groups to develop suggested rules, and the class votes for the rules to be accepted for use in the classroom.

Teacher Materials and Preparation

Have:
- Overhead projector
- Pen for marking on transparency

Make:
- Transparency of *Unacceptable Rules* (Box 9.1)
- Transparency of *Classroom Rules* (Box 9.2)
- Transparency of *Rules for Teacher* (Box 9.3)

Review:
- *Teacher Background Information* (Box 9.4)
- The section on contingency planning in Chapter 6

Key Information

If the classroom is to provide an environment for learning, it is important that each member of the class not only follows the rules, but also has a voice in creating them. Students are more likely to follow all the rules when they have had real input into developing some of them.

You do not have to accept every rule developed by the students. Rules that might negatively affect the learning process or do not fit your personality or teaching style should be eliminated. Explain why that rule cannot be used in these circumstances. Students usually know what rules fit a given classroom environment, and they are perfectly capable of developing many effective rules.

When students develop their own rules for the classroom, they are applying the principle of locus of control in a real-life situation. Thus, the classroom becomes a laboratory for learning responsible behavior.

Think of some examples of negative consequences for this activity, in case students have trouble thinking of their own.

Think about what restrictions you might want to use as guidelines for rule making.

Try to accept one or two classroom rules in the early discussion so students see you are serious about their concerns.

Procedure

Introduce the class to the concept of developing some of the classroom rules. Ask students to think of possible classroom benefits to the teacher and to students if students contribute to the classroom rules. Elicit as many benefits from the students as possible. Record the responses on the chalkboard.

Ask students to think of any possible drawbacks to their development of classroom rules. List these on the board.

Remind students of how contingency planning works (review this concept with them, if necessary; see Chapter 6). Elicit suggestions for eliminating or minimizing the possible drawbacks by planning for contingencies.

Explain again to students that you cannot accept every rule that is suggested. Give some restrictions as guidelines. Show the *Unacceptable Rules* transparency (Box 9.1). Tell students these are examples of rules you would not accept.

Show students the transparency of *Classroom Rules* (Box 9.2). Tell students these are examples of some possible rules. Divide the class into groups of four or five. Tell each group to think of three or four rules for all students to follow.

Explain that not every rule they create will actually be used. Students can be as creative as they want, as long as they truly believe their rules will make the classroom better for themselves and for you. If any of the contingency plans from Chapter 6 relate to the development of rules, point them out at this time.

After about fifteen minutes, ask one group to share its rules. Add the new rules to the transparency. Ask a second group to report. Record any new rules on the transparency. Continue until all the groups have reported. You should have each of the rules (with no duplicates) recorded on the transparency.

Tell students that they can select three or four rules for the class. Ask any student who wishes to make a case for or against any rule to do so, allowing one or two minutes.

Vote on the rules. Tell students they can vote, using a show of hands, for as many rules as they want. The three or four highest vote-getters will become the rules of the class. (Although more rules might apply, it is difficult to handle more than four rules. These should represent circumstances that come up often.)

Show students the *Rules for Teacher* transparency (Box 9.3). Explain that although it may sound a bit strange, you are going to give students a chance to think of a few rules for you to follow in the classroom. (Students are usually highly motivated by anything teachers do that is strange, as long as it doesn't threaten student safety.)

Ask students if they have any questions about the goal. Tell each group to think of three or four rules for you. Explain that all you want are rules, not consequences. (The number of rules is not etched in stone. About ten years of experience with this technique indicates that three or four rules is typical of most teachers who try it. Feel free to use the number that is most comfortable for you.)

After about fifteen minutes, ask one group to share its rules. Add the new rules to the transparency. Ask a second group to report. Record any new rules on the transparency. Continue until all the groups have reported.

Return the class to the large group. Ask if anyone can spot a rule that violates your list of restrictions. Cross off the list any rules the students find. Once the students have finished, go through the list yourself and eliminate any that you cannot live with, explaining your reasons. *Do not eliminate all of the rules or students will question your credibility. If absolutely necessary, rephrase some of the rules.*

If there are more than three or four rules left on the list, either choose your three favorites, or if they seem equally appealing to you, let students vote on their three favorites. You can also mix and match; you select two, and the students select two. By the end of the process, you should have three or four rules that you will feel comfortable following.

Tell students to record the classroom rules in their journals. Explain the consequences for breaking either the rules for students or for the teacher.

Evaluation

Tell students to record in their journals the results of the rules the class selected, both positive and negative, for a one-month period. In one month's time, ask students to share their opinions. Based on what they have learned about the rules, allow them to modify, eliminate, or add to the list of rules.

Many teachers prefer to ask a student or two to comment on a few rules each week.

Box 9.1   Unacceptable Rules

- Rules that violate school and class rules
- Rules that are against the law
- Rules that violate my values
- Rules that interfere with my goals and/or style of teaching

Box 9.2   Classroom Rules

- No copying
- No putdowns
- No interrupting when another is speaking
- No pushing or shoving in line

Box 9.3   Rules for Teacher

- No drinking coffee in class
- Be in class on time (not talking in the hall when the bell rings)
- Hand homework back on time
- No putdowns
- Do not embarrass a student in front of the rest of the class

Box 9.4   Teacher Background Information

Rules for a Classroom Community

Some teachers do not feel comfortable allowing students to think up classroom rules. My experience is that when students have a say in the rules, they feel more involved in the classroom dynamics and feel more empowered by the system. Everyone wins. If you have doubts, I suggest you give this a try. If you are sure this activity is not for you, then skip it.

Think of your reasons for having students develop rules for the classroom. You may or may not use these reasons, but the process will help you effectively teach this lesson.

Your reasons should be a personal statement, not a philosophical one. Draw on the sense of community in the classroom you are working to create.

One of the best ways to teach responsibility is to provide a model of it. A unique and effective technique for modeling responsibility is to allow students to develop rules for the teacher. As with the student rules, you do not have to accept every rule that the students develop. The typical rules that students want their teachers to follow are counterparts to what is asked of them. Remember, you are simply developing a few basic rules that indicate you value the opinions and needs of your students.

Giving students the right to develop rules for the teacher does not lead to loss of control or chaos, even though it may seem that way at first glance. It goes a long way toward developing a sense of responsibility in the class, and in the long run it makes teaching easier.

Teachers who have used this component from the *Discipline With Dignity* program report positive results

(continued)

Box 9.4 *(continued)*

that are meaningful and change the focus of the class to one of mutual respect based on shared experience.

I strongly suggest that you, rather than the students, be responsible for choosing the consequences of breaking a rule selected for you. The best response is the same for students: Develop a plan (in writing or orally) to change your behavior, and present your plan to the class. Once again, this technique allows you to model a behavior you expect from your students.

I suggest you intentionally break one of the student rules for you within the first two weeks of class. Let the students catch you. This provides a perfect opportunity for you to model the behavior that you expect from the students when they are caught breaking a classroom rule.

10

The Classroom as Community

Strategy Question 8: How do students create, recognize, and develop commitment to a classroom community?

Objectives

- Students will be able to identify elements of a classroom community.
- Students will synthesize an approach to make their classroom more of a community.
- Students will demonstrate personal commitment to the classroom as a community.

Time

Two class periods

Overview

This lesson is designed to help students think of their classroom as a community. Through various small-group activities, voting techniques, and group-development activities, students bring their ideas into action.

Teacher Materials and Preparation

Have:
- Overhead projector
- Pen for marking on transparency
- Newsprint or butcher paper and markers

Make:
Transparency of *Community* (Box 10.1)

Key Information

A sense of responsibility is increased when students feel they are active members of a community. When a classroom is perceived as only the teacher's or the school's, there is little commitment to a sense of responsibility for making it work. This lesson will help create that sense of community.

Students will explore the elements of a community in each of the following categories: family, club, gang, town, state, country, planet, and solar system. There are many school-based community groups that can be used as examples, including sports teams, tutoring groups, and programs for students who need special help or attention. (You may not need these examples, but if the students have trouble, you can use your list as examples.)

Classroom as community in a self-contained class (most elementary grades) is a natural. This also works well in block-scheduled or double-period classes. However, I first began using this technique twenty years ago in traditional forty- to fifty-minute classes and it worked very well.

Procedure

Ask students what the word *community* means. Ask for characteristics, benefits, or any other traits that define community. Show students the *Community* transparency (Box 10.1).

Record students' ideas about community on the transparency.

Tell students that your classroom can also be thought of as a community. Examine the lists on the transparency, and circle any characteristics of community that are true for a classroom.

Divide the class into groups of four or five. Ask each group to take ten minutes to think of what they can do to make the classroom more of a community than it currently is. Tell groups to think about contributions that anyone in class might make, not only their own personal ones.

Examples of possible contributions include the following:

Bring in posters for the wall.

Take turns bringing in snacks one day a week.

Help collect homework.

Set up a tutoring or study group so students can learn from each other.

If a bully is picking on a new student, escort the new student around school.

Correct each other's homework.

Establish a support group to talk over common problems. Publish a newsletter for parents and administrators about what is being learned in class. This can be done every four to six weeks and might only be two or three pages.

After ten minutes, ask groups to think of anything you as the teacher can do to make the classroom more of a community, based on the circled characteristics on the transparency. Allow ten minutes.

Ask groups to share their ideas for student contributions. Record the responses on butcher paper or a transparency. Continue until all groups have reported. Record each new idea on the paper.

Follow the same procedure for the ideas for you, the teacher.

Have students vote on the first set of ideas. Use 75 percent of the students as the deciding vote for either yes or no. This ensures that only the most popular ideas are chosen.

Select two to four of the ideas for you that you wish to incorporate into the classroom culture. (You may allow the students to vote on their favorite two to four ideas.)

Then ask students to leave the small groups and write in their journals about what they can do as individuals to make the classroom more of a community.

Divide the class into new groups, matching the number of groups to the number of ideas on the student list. Tell groups to use the planning skills from Chapter 6 to plan ways to make the ideas come to life in the classroom. Review these skills as appropriate.

Allow some class time over the next week or two for groups to complete their assignments. While students are working, you can also be looking for ways to incorporate their ideas for you into the classroom.

At the end of the development period, have groups make a presentation of their suggestions. Have the class vote yes or no on each group's suggestions. Use the 75 percent standard to determine which suggestions are accepted.

Present your suggestions on your ideas.

Over time, you can incorporate the accepted ideas into the way you and the students relate to each other in the classroom. This can be done as part of your everyday teaching, or as part of a bi-weekly or monthly class devoted to community process.

Evaluation

Ask students to record their individual ideas of community in their journals. Tell them to keep a record of how effective they are at actually putting their ideas into action in the classroom.

On one piece of paper, have students write a personal pledge that demonstrates their commitment to the classroom as a community. Perhaps make up a form on the computer using a large font, so there is one student pledge per page.

Example:

I, _____

pledge to _____ *to support*

(activity)

of my peers in this class.

Mount the pledges in the classroom and encourage students to read the pledges of others.

Box 10.1   Community

- School

- Friends

- City/Town

- State

- Country

- Planet

- Solar System

11

Conclusion

This book is an effort to make every classroom a welcoming place where teachers and students can work seriously and hard on important issues, materials, and activities. Without question, the teacher is always the final authority in the classroom, but the more students participate in establishing rules and conditions, the greater the stake they will feel in what happens in that classroom.

Learning about responsibility, control, prediction, planning, mistakes, and other areas covered in this book will give students a better sense of who they are and how to behave in a variety of circumstances and settings—not just in school. The more strategies students have for appropriate and effective behavior, the better they will be at every form of cooperation and learning.

Teachers may use all of the activities in this book or they may want to select only those chapters that fit their needs and personalities. The main point is to build the best learning community possible in every classroom by creating a setting where cooperation, respect, and dignity prevail. Time is precious in schools, and time spent on disruptive, non-productive behaviors is time taken from important learning.

This book represents Discipline With Dignity® and appropriate student involvement in classrooms where teachers and students are pleased to engage in important learning. I hope each reader has the success my efforts are intended to promote.

Glossary

Here are important terms and what I mean by them as used in this book.

Active Listening: Listening as if you are the person who is speaking, putting yourself in the speaker's shoes.

Aggression: Direct confrontation, showing how you feel directly to the person in conflict with you.

Community: A group of people with common values and/or goals or who come together for a common bond.

Contingency Planning: Including in the steps of a plan strategies for overcoming possible roadblocks or potential failure of the plan.

External Locus of Control: When control is outside of you. You cannot decide what will happen.

Internal Locus of Control: When control is inside you. You can decide what will happen.

Locus of Control: Place of control, where control resides.

Obedience: Doing what someone else tells you to do.

Passive Aggression: Indirect confrontation, showing how you feel with behaviors that are annoying or hurtful without directly communicating what the problem is.

Planning: Determining the steps needed to achieve a goal.

Predicting: Making an intelligent guess at what will happen.

Responsibility: Making choices, deciding for yourself.

Rules: The limits that must be enforced when broken. They describe behavior and are specific.

Values: The principles from which we identify rules. These are general and cannot be enforced.

Suggested Reading

Bar-Tal, D., & Bar-Zohay, Y. (1977, April). The relationship between perception of locus of control and academic achievement. *Contemporary Educational Psychology,* pp. 181–199.

Brendtro, L., Brokenleg, M., & VanBockern, S. (1990). *Reclaiming youth at risk.* Bloomington, IN: National Educational Service.

Brendtro, L., Ness, A., & Mitchell, M. (2001). *No disposable kids.* Longmont, CO: Sopris West.

Carlson, R. (1997). *Don't sweat the small stuff.* New York: Hyperion.

Csikszentmihalyi, M. (1990). *Flow: The psychology of optimal experience.* New York: Harper & Row.

Curwin, R. (1992). *Rediscovering Hope: Our greatest teaching strategy.* Bloomington, IN: National Educational Service.

Curwin, R., & Mendler, A. (1988). *Discipline with dignity.* Alexandria, VA: Association for Supervision and Curriculum Development.

Curwin, R., & Mendler, A. (1990). *Am I in trouble?* Santa Cruz, CA: ETR Associates.

Curwin, R., & Mendler, A. (1997). *As tough as necessary: Countering violence, aggression, and hostility in our schools.* Alexandria, VA: Association of Supervision and Curriculum Development.

Curwin, R., & Mendler, A. (1999). *Discipline with dignity* (2nd ed.). Alexandria, VA: Association for Supervision and Curriculum Development.

DeCharms, R. (1968). *Personal causation: The internal affective determinants of behavior.* New York: Academic Press.

Glasser, W. (1986). *Control theory in the classroom.* New York: Harper & Row.

Long, N., & Long, J. (2001). *Managing passive-aggressive behavior of children at school and home.* Austin, TX: Pro-Ed.

Mendler, A. (1992). *What do I do when . . .? How to achieve discipline with dignity in the classroom.* Bloomington, IN: National Educational Service.

Mendler, A. (1997). *Power struggles.* Rochester, NY: Discipline Associates.

Mendler, A. (2000). *Motivating students who don't care.* Bloomington, IN: National Educational Service.

Mendler, A. (2001). *Connecting with students.* Alexandria, VA: Association of Supervision and Curriculum Development.

Mendler, A. N. (1990). *Smiling at yourself.* Santa Cruz, CA: ETR Associates.

Mendler, A., & Curwin, R. (1999). *Discipline with dignity for challenging youth.* Bloomington, IN: National Educational Service.

Philliber, S. (1995). *A "what works" report: Supporting effective youth development programs.* St. Louis, MO: Metropolitan Association for Philanthropy.

Prager, D. (1995). *Think a second time.* New York: HarperCollins.

Sagor, R. (1996, September). Building resiliency in students. *Educational Leadership, 54*(1).

Seita, J., & Brendtro, L. (2002). *Kids who outwit adults.* Longmont, CO: Sopris West.

Wood, M., & Long, N. (1991). *Life space intervention.* Austin, TX: Pro-ed.

Index